Introduction

PATTERN

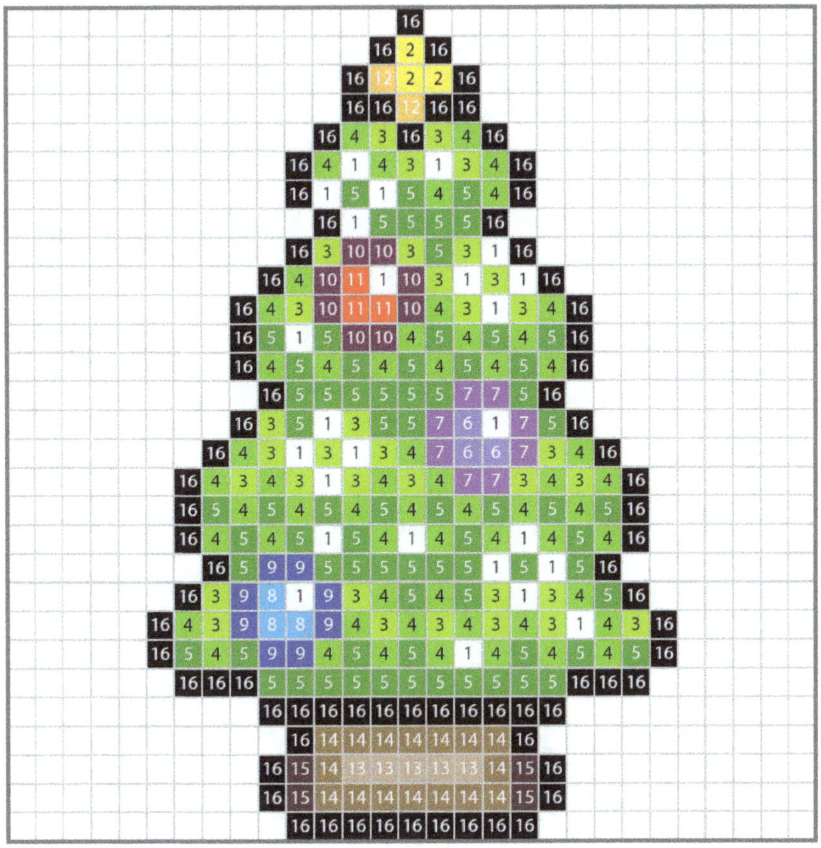

EXAMPLE

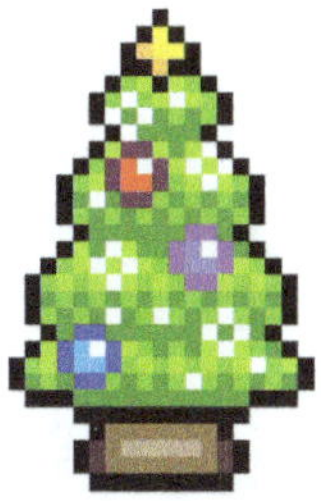

COLOR INDEX

	Color	#
1	White	25
2	Yellow	3
3	Kiwi Lime	34
4	Green	59
5	Dark Green	72
6	Pastel Lavander	3
7	Plum	8
8	Turquoise	3
9	Dark Blue	8
10	Cranapple	8
11	Red	3
12	Cheddar	2
13	Tan	5
14	Light Brown	16
15	Brown	4
16	Black	80

LOCATION IN PATTERN
COLOR OF BEAD
 # OF BEADS NEEDED

Beadcraft patterns use a simple color-by-numbers format. For instance, if you're making the Christmas Tree above, you'll need 25 white beads, each corresponding to the locations marked with the number **1** in the pattern, three yellow beads that correspond to number **2**, 34 kiwi lime (or light green) beads that correspond to number **3**, and so on. The colors referenced in the patterns are based on the Perler Bead brand. If you're using a different type of fusion bead—no problem! Simply substitute a similar color to follow the pattern.

Use these patterns as a guide, but don't be afraid to try new color combinations or make your own designs. Each pattern has a border of black beads. However, to simplify the designs, you may leave off the border.

© 2016 Johnathan Roy
All Rights Reserved.

Classic Christmas

COLOR INDEX

1		White	83
2		Gray	77
3		Red	47
4		Peach	12
5		Cranapple	54
6		Sand	19
7		Tan	12
8		Dark Green	14
9		Green	7
10		Yellow	2
11		Dark Blue	2
12		Black	106

COLOR INDEX

1		White	14
2		Yellow	56
3		Green	47
4		Red	191
5		Black	135

COLOR INDEX

1		White	25
2		Yellow	3
3		Kiwi Lime	34
4		Green	59
5		Dark Green	72
6		Pastel Lavander	3
7		Plum	8
8		Turquoise	3
9		Dark Blue	8
10		Cranapple	8
11		Red	3
12		Cheddar	2
13		Tan	5
14		Light Brown	16
15		Brown	4
16		Black	80

COLOR INDEX

1		White	2
2		Tan	27
3		Gold Metallic	47
4		Brown	104
5		Cranapple	13
6		Red	5
7		Dark Green	38
8		Green	30
9		Kiwi Lime	16
10		Black	162

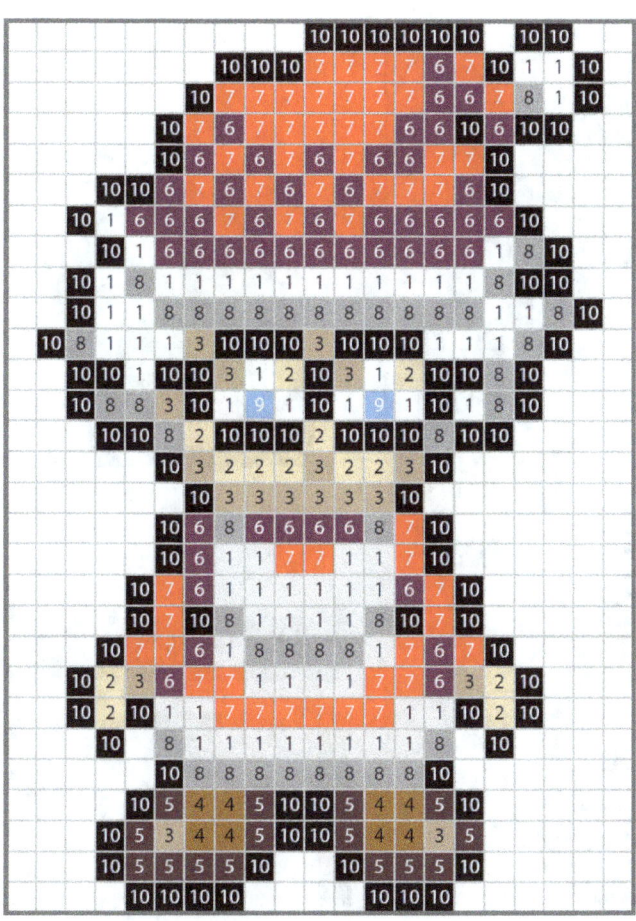

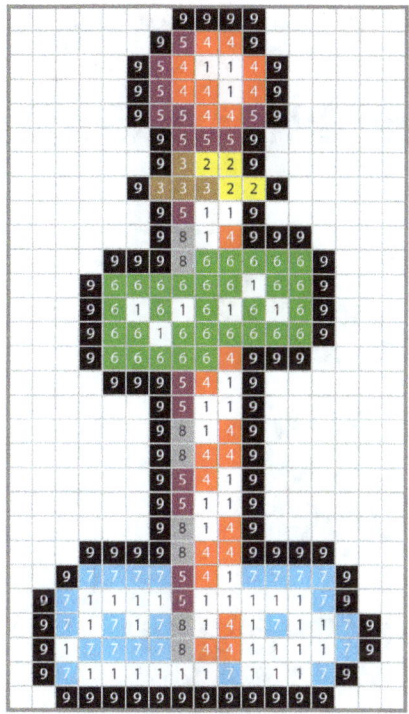

COLOR INDEX

1	White	68
2	Sand	13
3	Tan	18
4	Gold Metallic	8
5	Brown	15
6	Cranapple	50
7	Red	55
8	Pearl Silver	42
9	Pastel Blue	2
10	Black	108

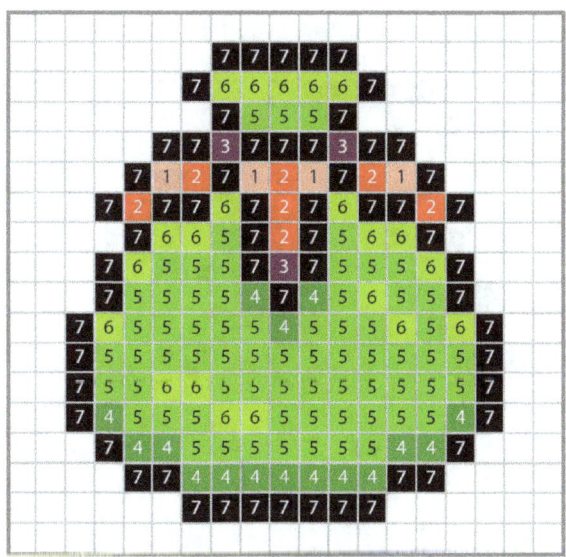

COLOR INDEX

1	Peach	4
2	Red	7
3	Cranapple	3
4	Dark Green	16
5	Green	67
6	Kiwi Lime	21
7	Black	60

COLOR INDEX

1	White	50
2	Yellow	4
3	Light Brown	4
4	Red	23
5	Cranapple	16
6	Dark Green	31
7	Turquoise	23
8	Pearl Silver	8
9	Black	84

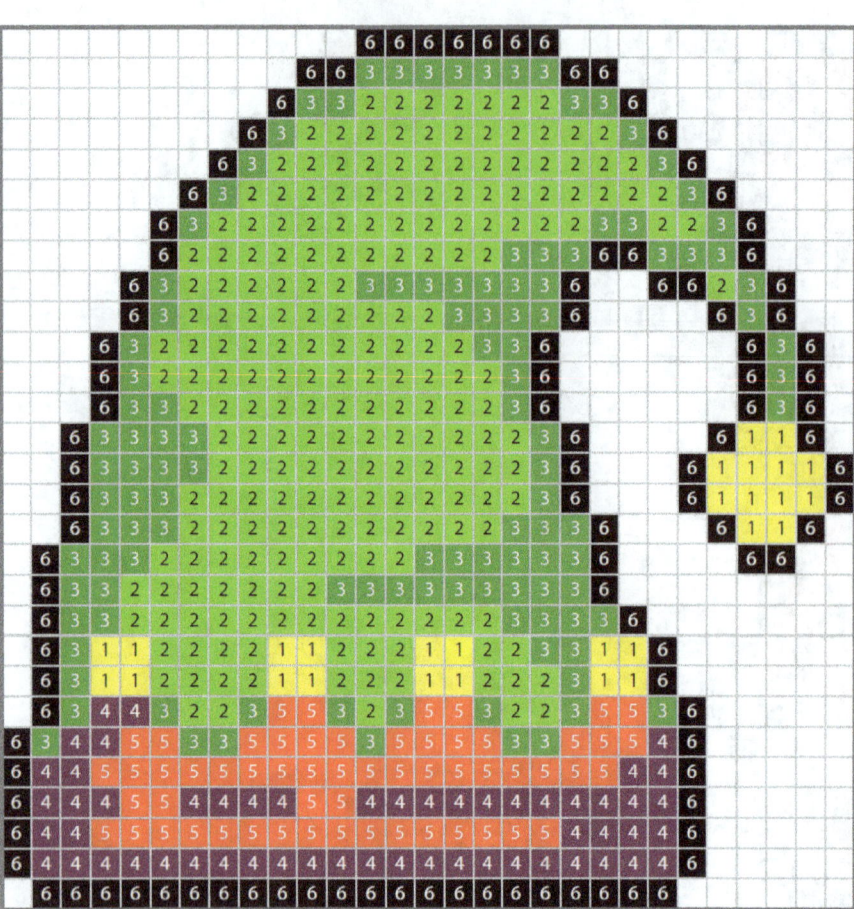

COLOR INDEX

1	Yellow	27
2	Green	220
3	Dark Green	118
4	Cranapple	55
5	Red	57
6	Black	108

COLOR INDEX

1	White	8
2	Yellow	6
3	Sand	48
4	Tan	7
5	Light Brown	27
6	Brown	15
7	Cranapple	24
8	Red	28
9	Green	75
10	Dark Green	47
11	Turquoise	2
12	Black	94

COLOR INDEX

1	White	41
2	Pearl Silver	21
3	Dark Grey	42
4	Cranapple	16
5	Magenta	6
6	Red	111
7	Rust	77
8	Dark Green	15
9	Green	12
10	Kiwi Lime	10
11	Black	116

COLOR INDEX

1	White	49
2	Toothpaste	45
3	Sky Blue	57
4	Peach	49
5	Red	91
6	Rust	90
7	Black	89

This design is larger than a standard 29 x 29 board.

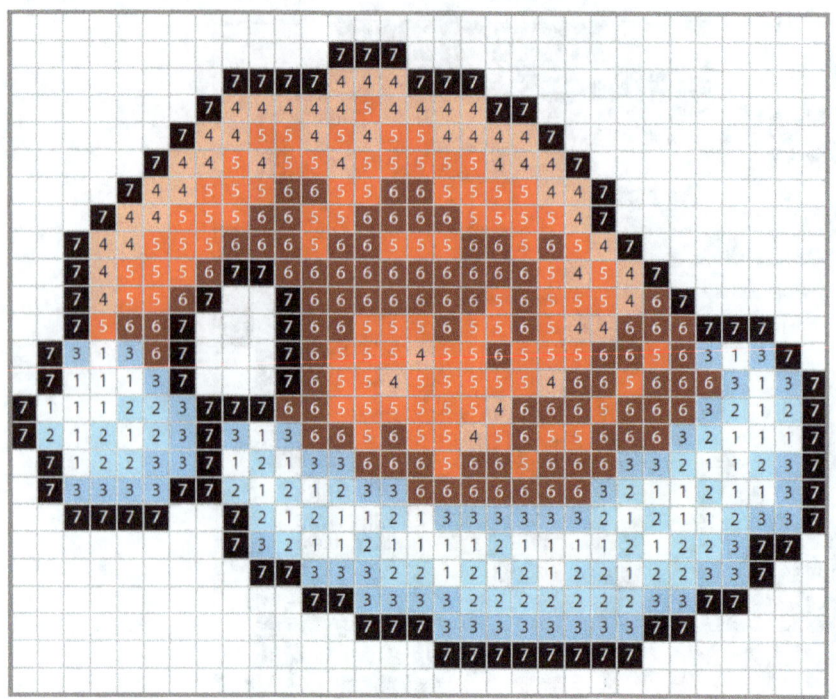

COLOR INDEX

1	White	17
2	Sand	67
3	Tan	93
4	Light Brown	63
5	Brown	60
6	Red	3
7	Peach	1
8	Black	152

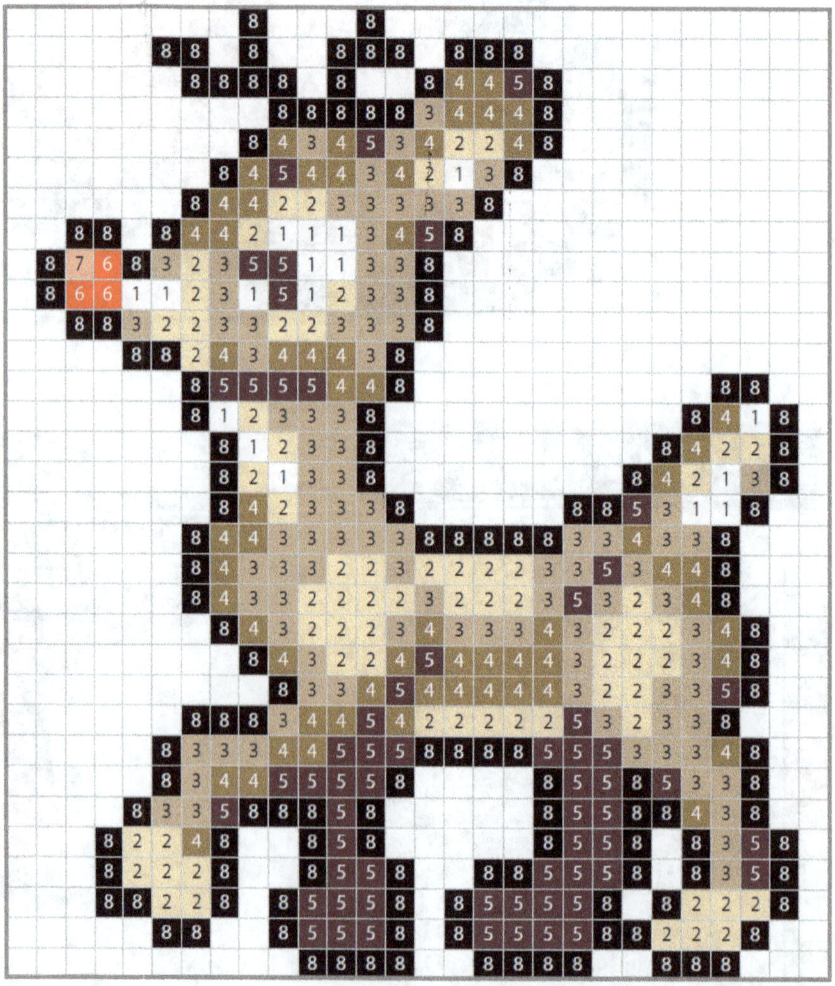

This design is larger than a standard 29 x 29 board.

Christmas Decorations

This design is larger than a standard 29 x 29 board.

COLOR INDEX

#	Color	Count
1	White	10
2	Yellow	18
3	Tan	30
4	Peach	19
5	Red	81
6	Cranapple	96
7	Dark Green	109
8	Green	41
9	Brown	4
10	Black	218

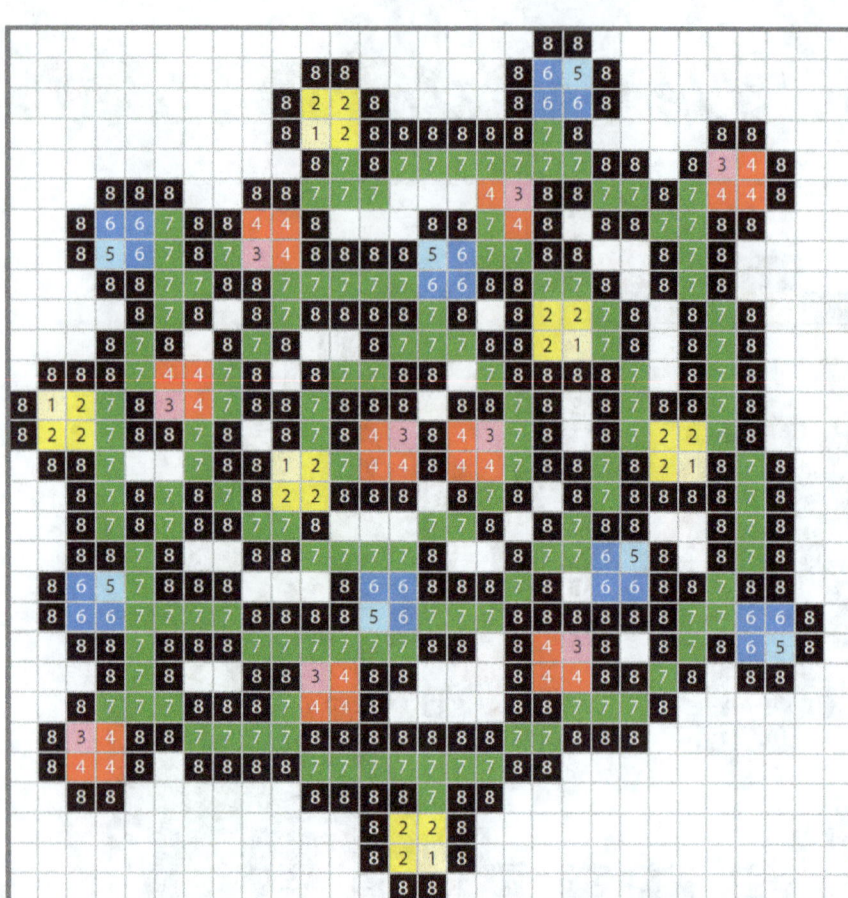
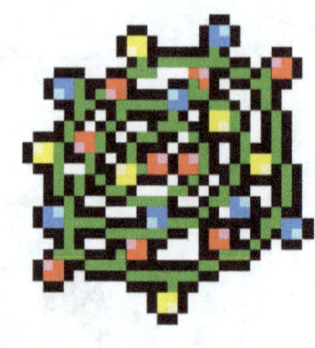

COLOR INDEX

1	Creme	6
2	Yellow	18
3	Light Pink	9
4	Red	26
5	Toothpaste	7
6	Light Blue	21
7	Dark Green	136
8	Black	262

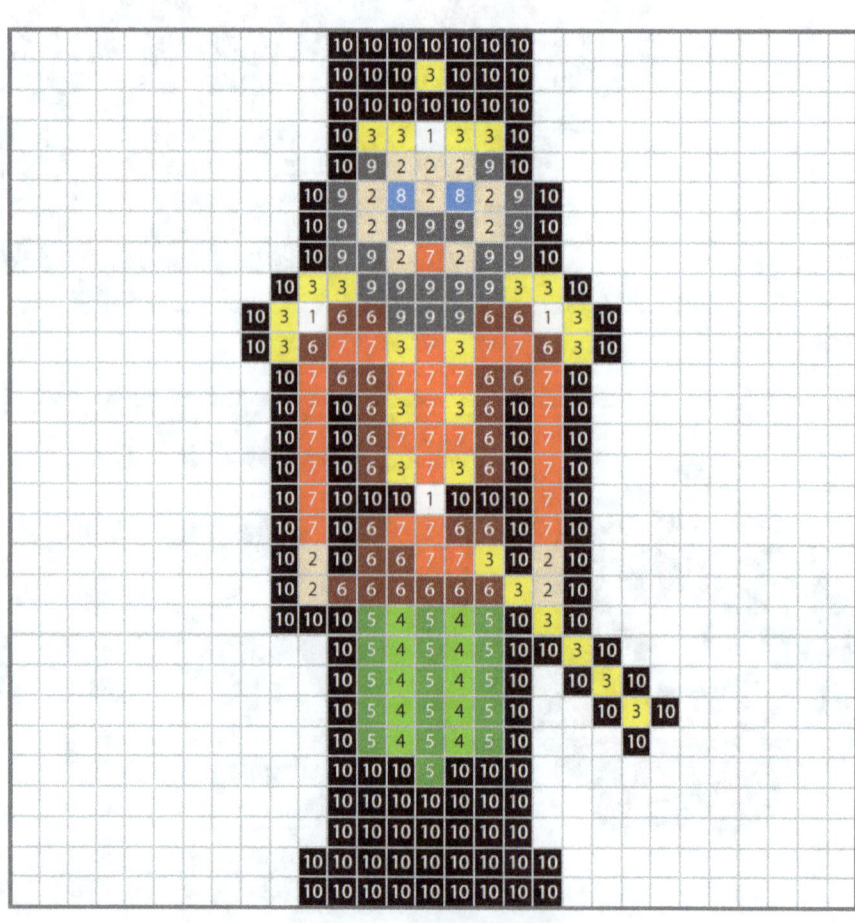

COLOR INDEX

1	White	4
2	Sand	14
3	Yellow	25
4	Green	10
5	Dark Green	16
6	Cranapple	27
7	Red	30
8	Light Blue	2
9	Dark Grey	21
10	Black	126

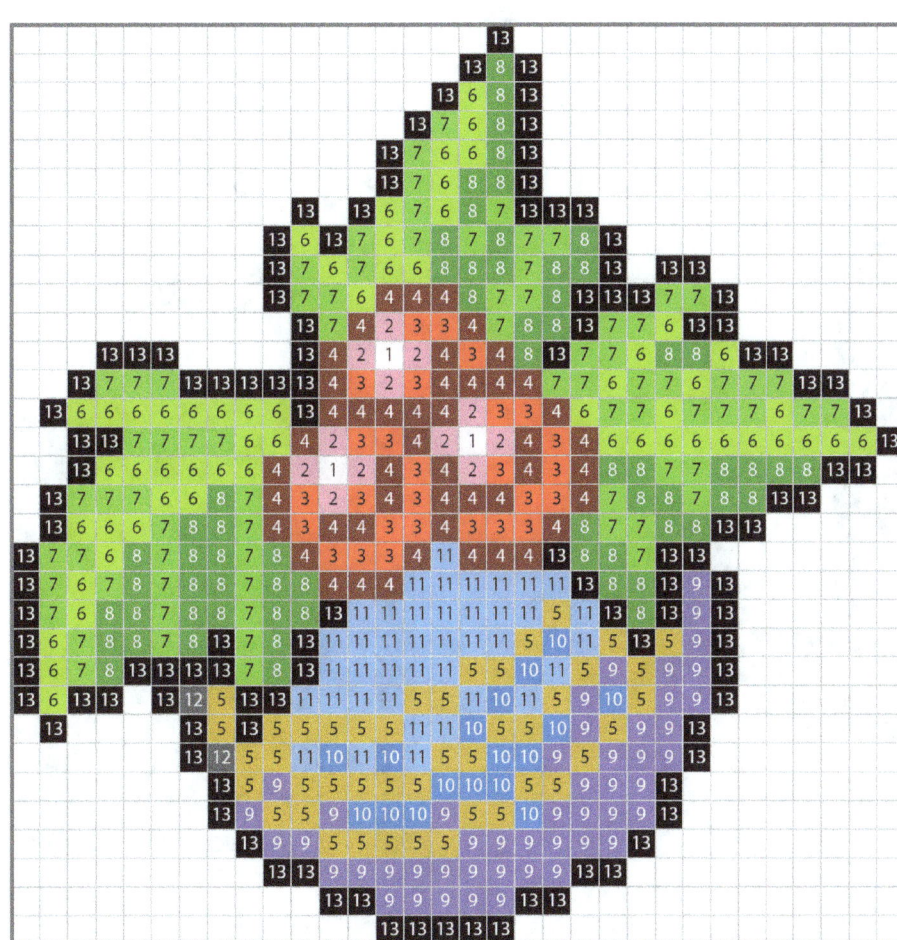

The designs on this page are larger than a standard 29 x 29 board.

COLOR INDEX

1		White	3
2		Light Pink	12
3		Red	27
4		Rust	47
5		Gold Pearl	44
6		Kiwi Lime	58
7		Green	75
8		Dark Green	64
9		Grape	49
10		Light Blue	17
11		Pastel Blue	40
12		Dark Grey	2
13		Black	119

COLOR INDEX

1		White	32
2		Creme	4
3		Yellow	44
4		Cheddar	53
5		Butterscotch	44
6		Brown	20
7		Rust	87
8		Cranapple	23
9		Red	17
10		Hot Coral	23
11		Light Pink	15
12		Kiwi Lime	20
13		Green	36
14		Dark Green	40
15		Black	120

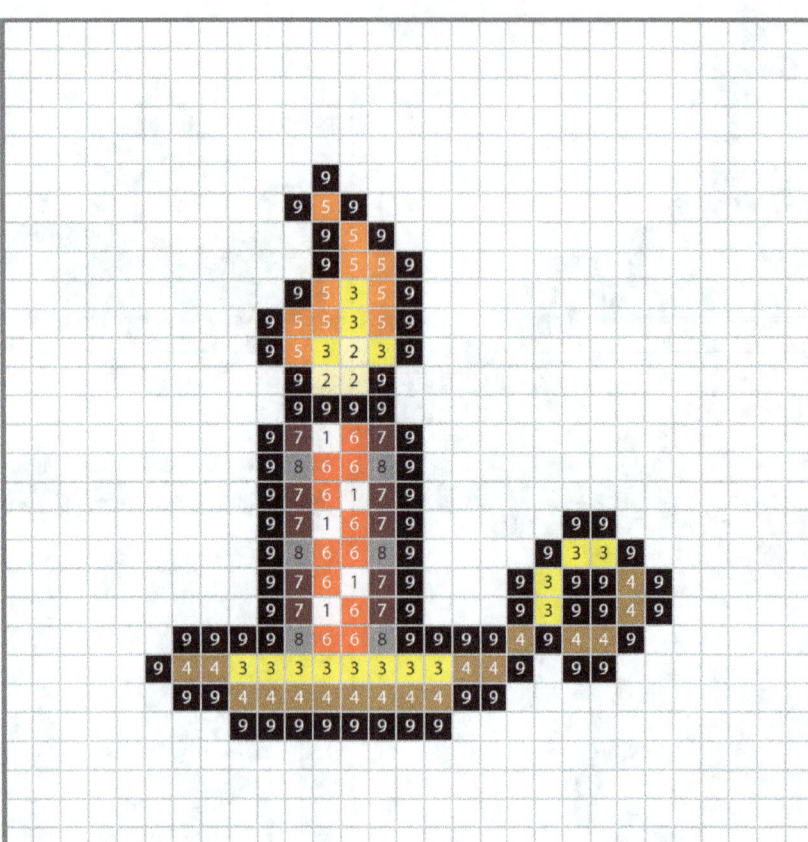

COLOR INDEX

1	White	5
2	Creme	3
3	Yellow	16
4	Light Brown	17
5	Orange	10
6	Red	11
7	Rust	10
8	Grey	6
9	Black	71

COLOR INDEX

1	White	11
2	Yellow	16
3	Butterscotch	4
4	Magenta	170
5	Cranapple	25
6	Dark Green	36
7	Green	129
8	Kiwi Lime	4
9	Grey	6
10	Dark Grey	9
11	Black	82

This design is larger than a standard 29 x 29 board.

COLOR INDEX

#	Color	Count
1	White	29
2	Yellow	12
3	Cheddar	24
4	Peach	15
5	Red	32
6	Rust	63
7	Light Blue	51
8	Pastel Blue	46
9	Green	53
10	Dark Green	187
11	Pearl Silver	23
12	Black	162

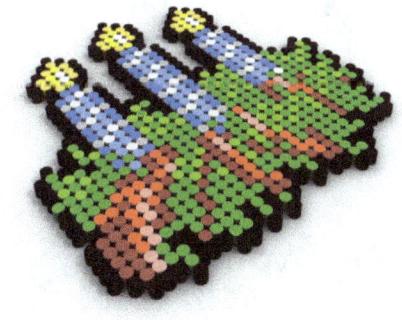

COLOR INDEX

1	White	24
2	Cheddar	65
3	Light Brown	49
4	Black	152

COLOR INDEX

1	Red	67
2	Cranapple	91
3	Black	147

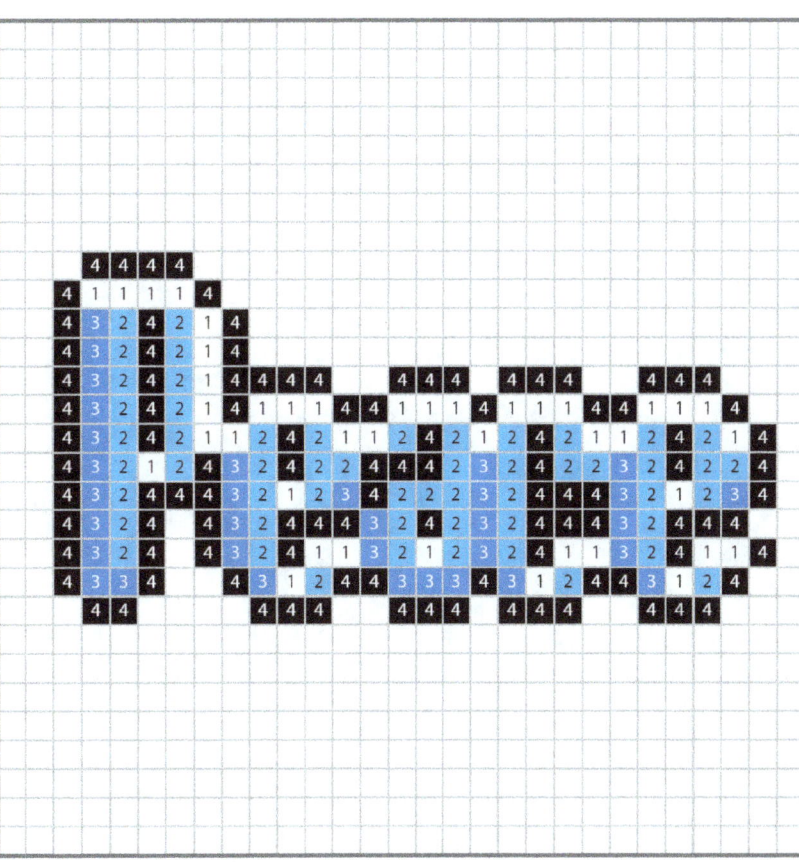

COLOR INDEX

1	White	41
2	Turquoise	54
3	Light Blue	33
4	Black	104

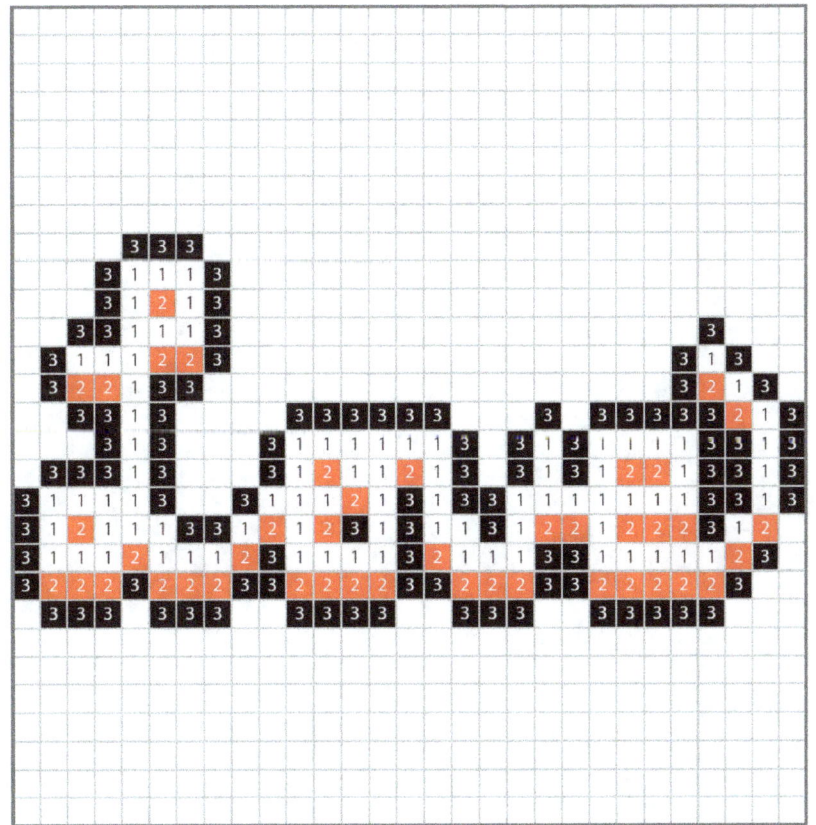

COLOR INDEX

1	White	85
2	Red	43
3	Black	105

Christmas Treats

COLOR INDEX

1	White	45
2	Pearl Silver	30
3	Red	53
4	Cranapple	54
5	Black	80

COLOR INDEX

1	White	11
2	Pearl Silver	10
3	Red	19
4	Cranapple	21
5	Brown	9
6	Black	40

COLOR INDEX

1	White	13	
2	Sand	21	
3	Tan	203	
4	Light Brown	76	
5	Brown	71	
6	Rust	8	
7	Raspberry Pearl	10	
8	Red	3	
9	Peach	1	
10	Kiwi Lime	1	
11	Green	3	
12	Dark Green	8	
13	Pearl Silver	5	
14	Black	95	

This design is larger than a standard 29 x 29 board.

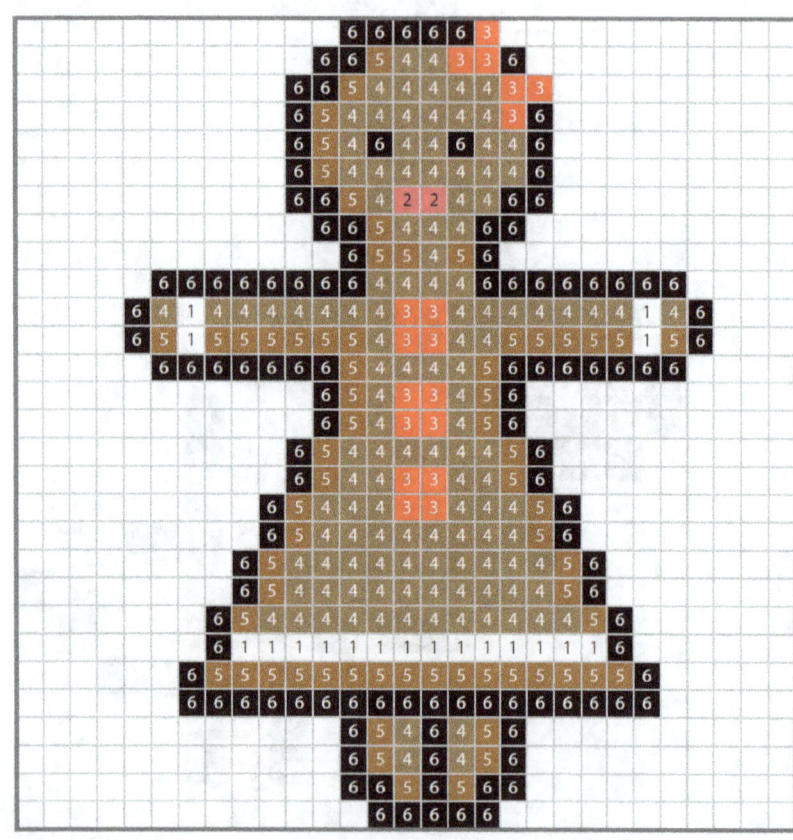

COLOR INDEX

1	White	18	
2	Hot Coral	2	
3	Red	18	
4	Light Brown	123	
5	Gold Metallic	65	
6	Black	118	

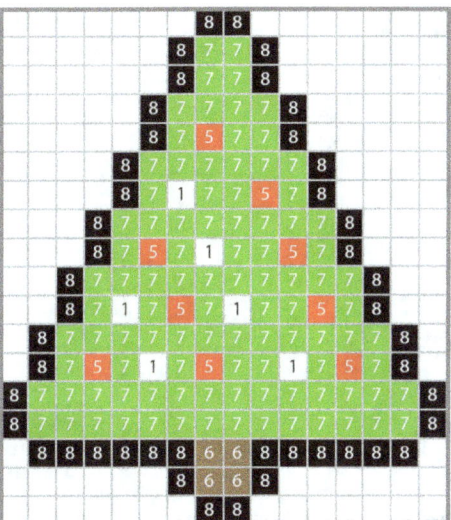
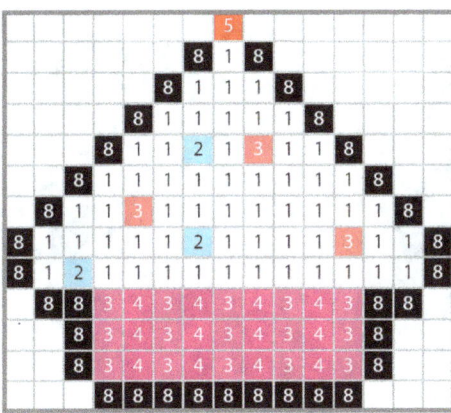
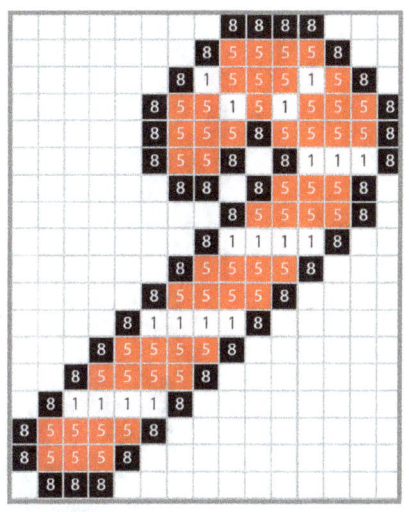

COLOR INDEX

1	White	81
2	Toothpaste	3
3	Light Pink	18
4	Pink	12
5	Red	63
6	Light Brown	4
7	Green	97
8	Black	122

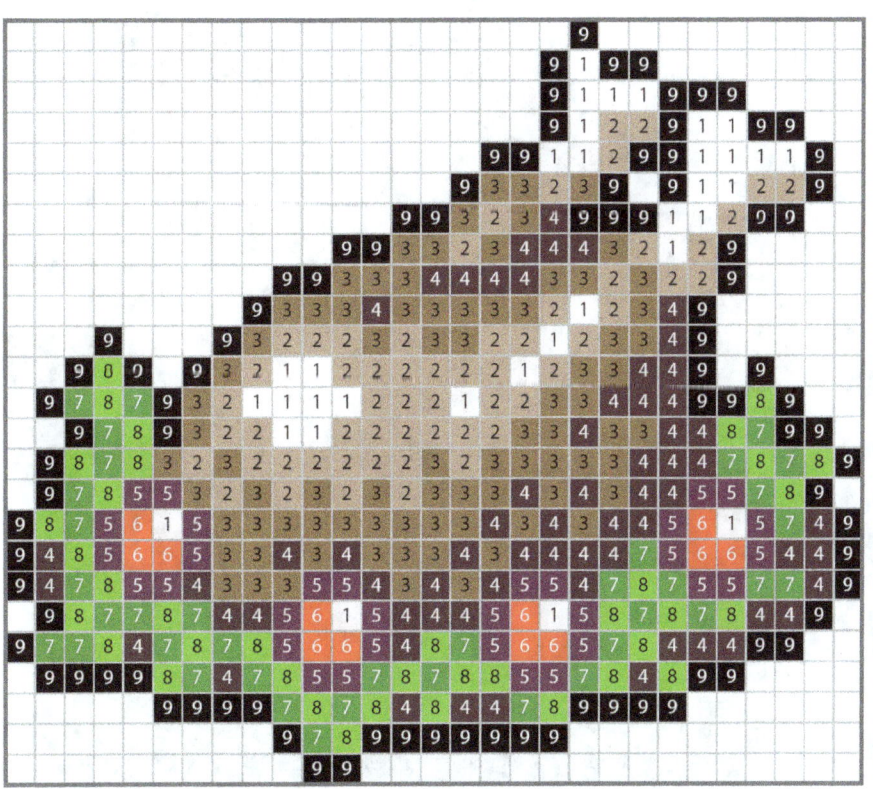
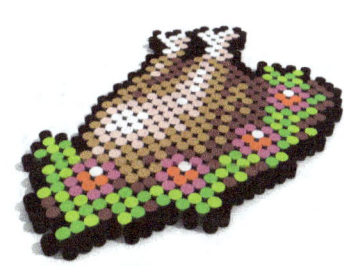

COLOR INDEX

1	White	34
2	Tan	57
3	Light Brown	81
4	Brown	66
5	Cranapple	32
6	Red	12
7	Dark Green	37
8	Green	37
9	Black	92

COLOR INDEX

1	White	51
2	Pearl Light Blue	59
3	Pastel Blue	57
4	Green	12
5	Red	4
6	Magenta	37
7	Cranapple	1
8	Black	78

COLOR INDEX

1	White	85
2	Pearl Light Blue	40
3	Parrot Green	38
4	Green	78
5	Light Brown	241
6	Rust	62
7	Red	49
8	Hot Coral	8
9	Black	87

O Holy Night

COLOR INDEX

1	White	66
2	Yellow	32
3	Toothpaste	60
4	Pastel Blue	195
5	Light Blue	45
6	Hot Coral	2
7	Peach	2
8	Sand	50
9	Black	104

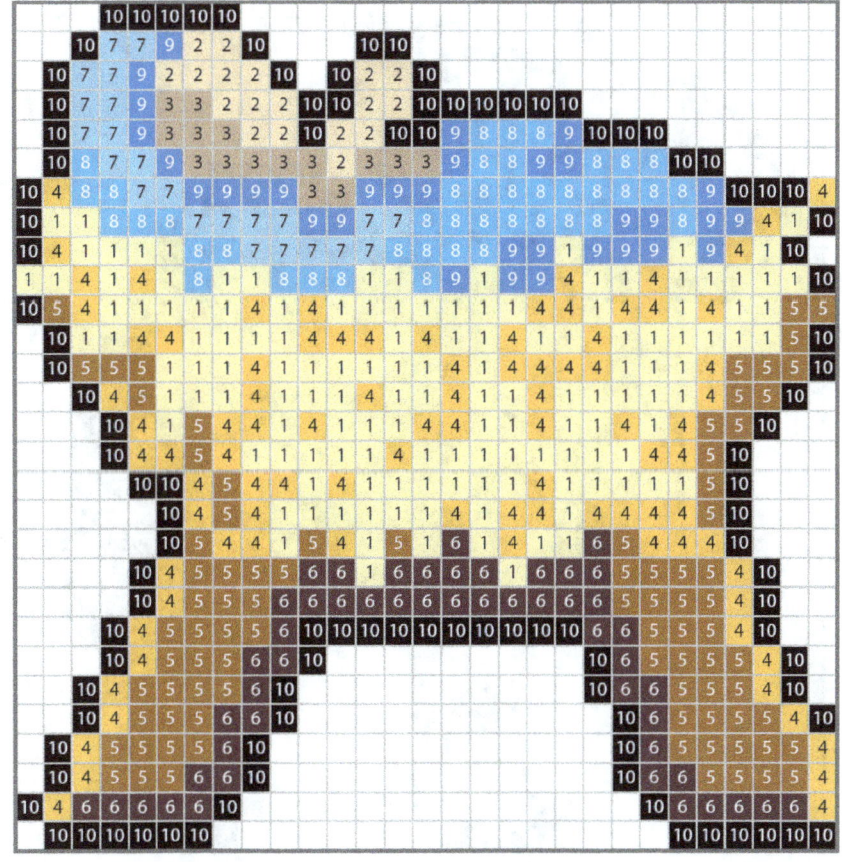

COLOR INDEX

1	Creme	139
2	Sand	18
3	Tan	15
4	Cheddar	92
5	Gold Metallic	85
6	Brown	51
7	Sky Blue	23
8	Turquoise	42
9	Light Blue	33
10	Black	108

COLOR INDEX

1	White	46
2	Toothpaste	3
3	Pastel Blue	16
4	Light Blue	51
5	Dark Blue	2
6	Light Brown	16
7	Sand	9
8	Pearl Silver	33
9	Dark Grey	37
10	Black	102

COLOR INDEX

1	White	3
2	Tan	45
3	Light Brown	117
4	Brown	108
5	Red	22
6	Dark Green	27
7	Grey	17
8	Black	134

COLOR INDEX

1	Sand	32
2	Yellow	8
3	Cheddar	8
4	Butterscotch	10
5	Gold Metallic	9
6	Light Brown	47
7	Brown	14
8	Cranapple	34
9	Red	29
10	Hot Coral	5
11	Peach	4
12	Pastel Lavander	18
13	Purple	58
14	Grape	32
15	Periwinkle Blue	52
16	Dark Blue	57
17	Dark Green	19
18	Green	12
19	Kiwi Lime	16
20	Dark Grey	30
21	Black	192

Christmas Gifts

COLOR INDEX

1	Toothpaste	30
2	Pastel Blue	149
3	Light Blue	110
4	Dark Blue	17
5	Cranapple	5
6	Magenta	55
7	Pink	61
8	Light Pink	14
9	Black	90

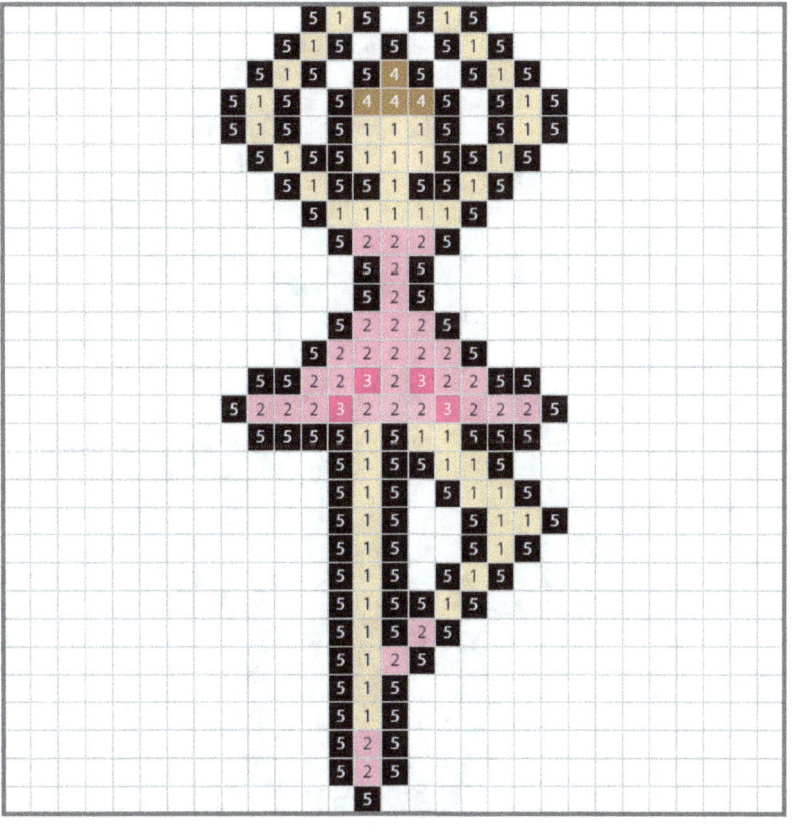

COLOR INDEX

1	Sand	48
2	Light Pink	31
3	Pink	4
4	Light Brown	4
5	Black	103

COLOR INDEX

#	Color	Count
1	Creme	23
2	Cheddar	8
3	Peach	1
4	Blush	8
5	Red	10
6	Cranapple	17
7	Light Brown	19
8	Pearl Silver	17
9	Dark Grey	37
10	Black	80

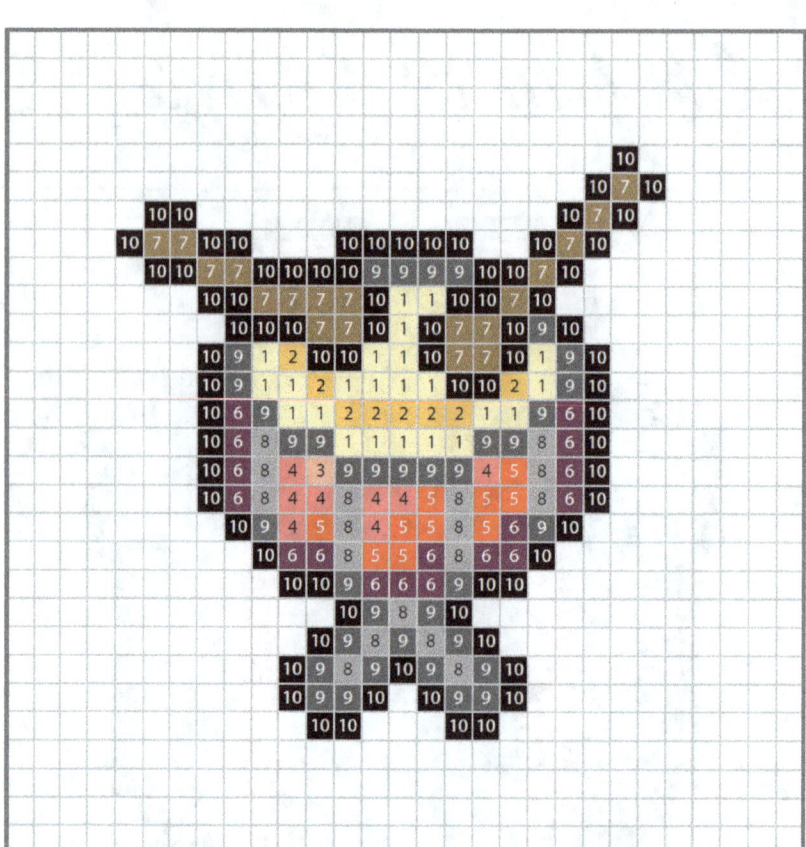

COLOR INDEX

#	Color	Count
1	Sand	36
2	Pink	27
3	Light Brown	22
4	Pastel Green	12
5	Parrot Green	14
6	Dark Green	34
7	Green	110
8	Black	109

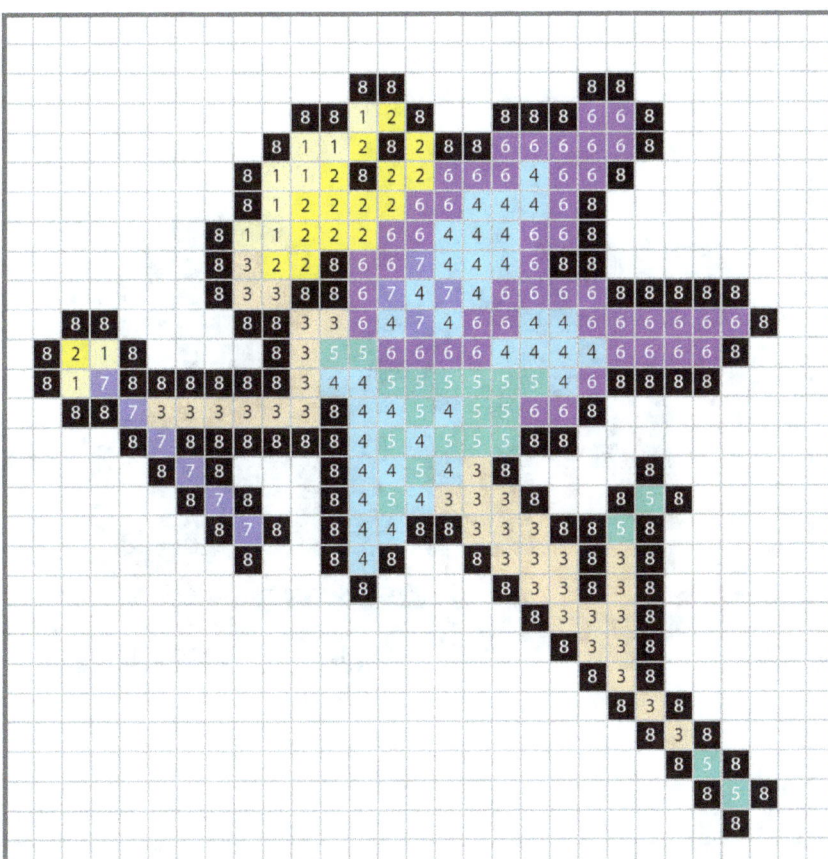

COLOR INDEX

1	Creme	10
2	Yellow	16
3	Sand	35
4	Toothpaste	36
5	Parrot Green	21
6	Plum	47
7	Pastel Lavander	10
8	Black	112

COLOR INDEX

1	White	32
2	Yellow	3
3	Sand	22
4	Raspberry	1
5	Red	42
6	Cranapple	23
7	Dark Blue	2
8	Grey	6
9	Black	103

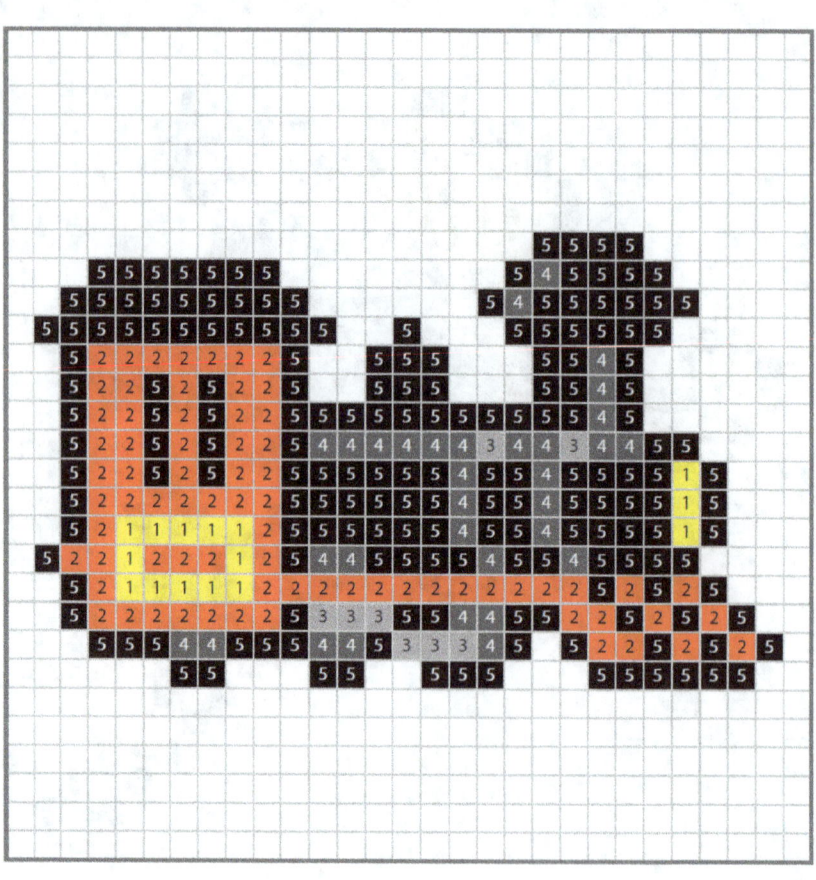

COLOR INDEX

1	Yellow	15
2	Red	72
3	Pearl Silver	8
4	Dark Grey	32
5	Black	183

COLOR INDEX

1	Creme	8
2	Yellow	43
3	Peach	11
4	Hot Coral	60
5	Red	53
6	Butterscotch	32
7	Kiwi Lime	26
8	Green	106
9	Dark Green	97
10	Light Brown	4
11	Rust	4
12	Black	86

Winter Wonderland

This design is larger than a standard 29 x 29 board.

COLOR INDEX

#	Color	Count
1	White	136
2	Toothpaste	88
3	Pastel Blue	54
4	Peach	10
5	Blush	20
6	Red	28
7	Raspberry Pearl	3
8	Rust	38
9	Light Brown	19
10	Butterscotch	3
11	Cheddar	4
12	Yellow	2
13	Kiwi Lime	23
14	Green	35
15	Dark Green	41
16	Black	119

COLOR INDEX

1	White	10
2	Pearl Light Blue	19
3	Pastel Blue	19
4	Light Blue	45
5	Dark Blue	41
6	Dark Grey	42
7	Grey	14
8	Pearl Silver	19
9	Black	101

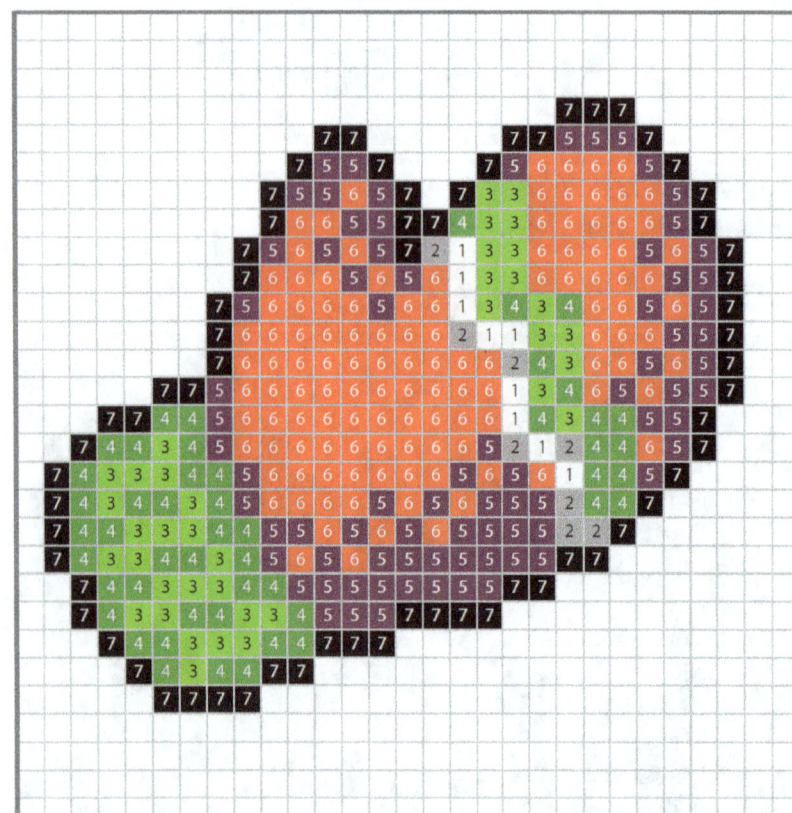

COLOR INDEX

1	White	9
2	Pearl Silver	8
3	Green	38
4	Dark Green	49
5	Cranapple	79
6	Red	119
7	Black	67

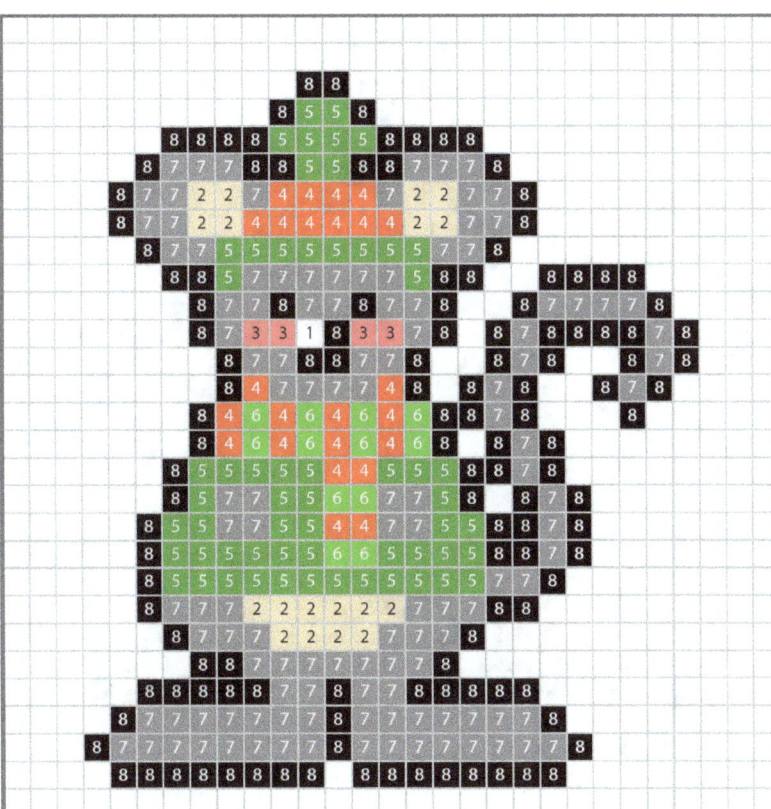

COLOR INDEX

1	White	1
2	Sand	18
3	Blush	4
4	Red	23
5	Dark Green	58
6	Green	12
7	Grey	121
8	Black	129

COLOR INDEX

1	Creme	6
2	Yellow	20
3	Cheddar	30
4	Gold Metallic	176
5	Brown	161
6	Cranapple	139
7	Red	5
8	Green	24
9	Dark Green	37
10	Black	102

COLOR INDEX

1	White	12
2	Creme	48
3	Yellow	79
4	Cheddar	46
5	Orange	51
6	Black	92

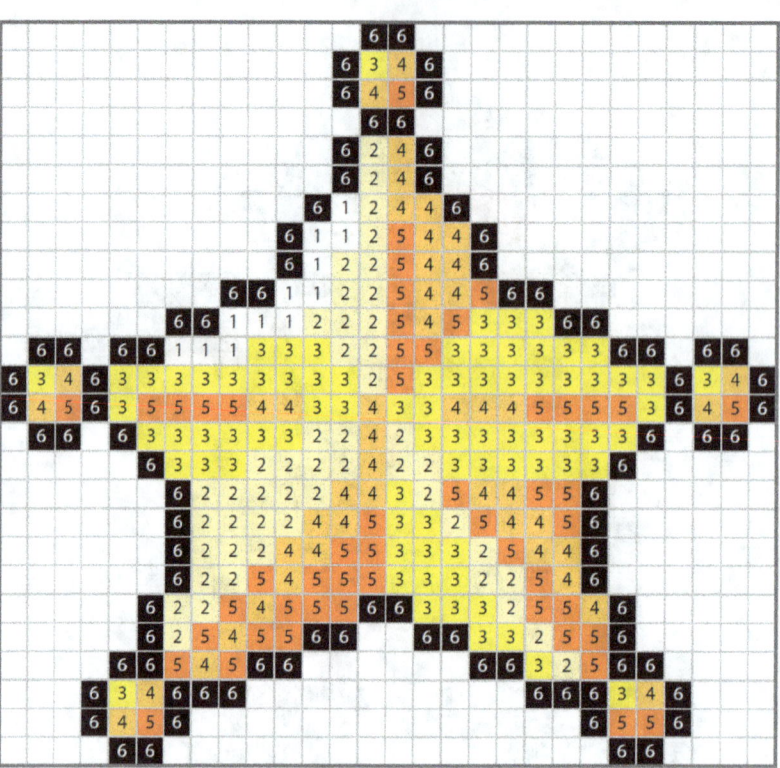

COLOR INDEX

1	White	143
2	Pastel Blue	123
3	Black	240

COLOR INDEX

1	White	84
2	Pearl Light Blue	12
3	Green	121
4	Dark Green	21
5	Brown	8
6	Light Brown	12
7	Black	102

COLOR INDEX

1	Green	1
2	Dark Green	18
3	Red	4
4	Cranapple	23
5	Black	58

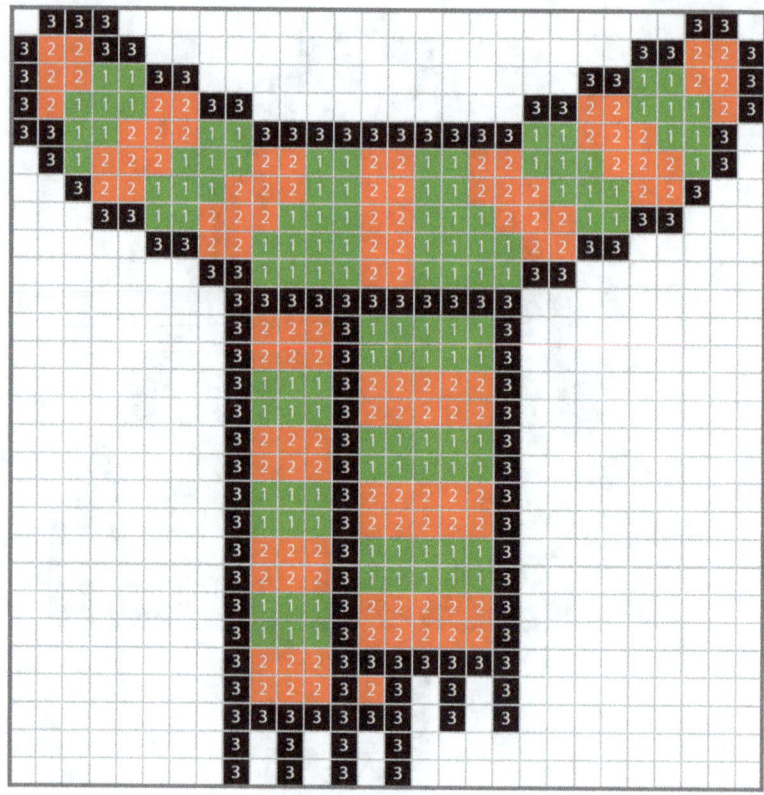

COLOR INDEX

1	Red	114
2	Green	115
3	Black	129

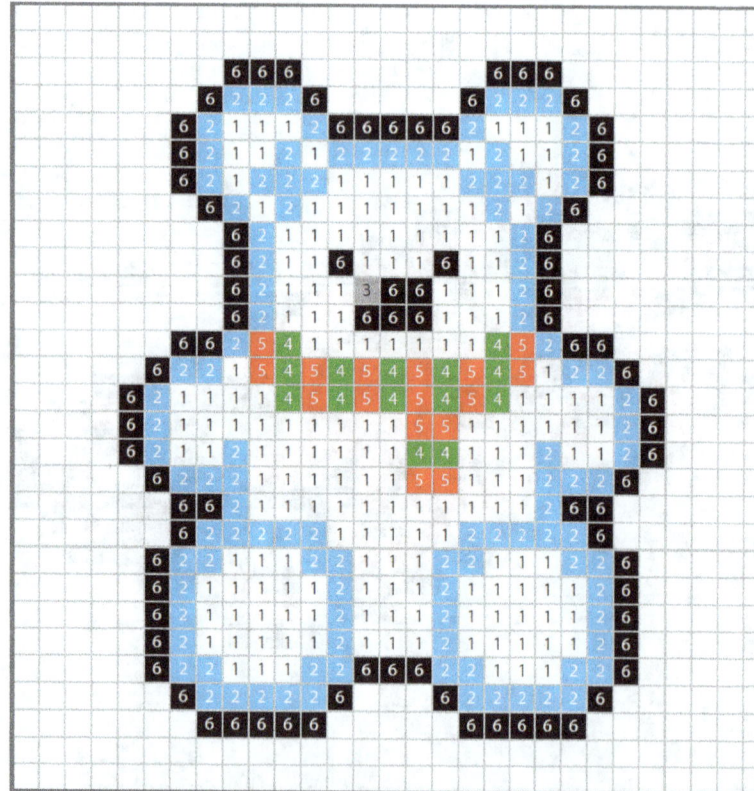

COLOR INDEX

1	White	180
2	Pearl Silver	109
3	Turquoise	1
4	Dark Green	14
5	Red	16
6	Black	85